Consecrated
IN HIM

30 Day Devotional

Peta Taberner

Consecrated IN HIM

30 Day Devotional

Peta Taberner

Consecrated
IN HIM

30 Day Devotional

Consecrated IN HIM is a 30-day devotional but is more than just a reading plan— it's a journey of intimacy, identity, and transformation in Christ.
Each day will draw you closer to the heart of the Father and deepen your walk as you become more like Jesus.
Take your time, be intentional, and allow the Holy Spirit to speak, heal, and shape you.

Consecrated
IN HIM

30 Day Devotional

IN HIM Day 1 - 10
Chosen, Accepted, Made New, Loved, Secure,
Complete, Hidden, Known, Intimacy, Abide

CONSECRATED Day 11 - 20
Set Apart, Cleansed, Sanctified, Made Holy,
Refined, Purified, Sacrifice, Renewed, Disciplined,
Surrendered

TRANSFORMED & EMPOWERED Day 21 - 30
Established, Confident, Purpose, Strengthened,
Fruitful, Overflow, Bold, Perseverance,
Commissioned, Fullness

IN HIM

Day 1 *Chosen*

Scripture: Ephesians 1:4 (AMP)

"just as [in His love] He chose us in Christ [actually selected us for Himself as His own] before the foundation of the world, so that we would be holy [that is, consecrated, set apart for Him, purpose-driven] and blameless in His sight."

Devotion:
Before you ever pursued God, He chose you and set His love upon you. Your life begins from belonging, not striving. You are His by intention, not accident. The meaning and definition of the word "chose" means; to want, to desire, to prefer, to select, to favour, to adopt, elect. The word chosen that the bible uses for us is the same word it uses for Jesus- the elect, the chosen of God.
You have been chosen, hand-picked by God Himself to be fully His. When you truly receive this revelation, consecration becomes your response, not your requirement, as you give your life back to the One who first chose you.

Day 1 *Chosen*

Reflection 1: Do I truly believe God has chosen me personally?

____
____
____
____
____
____

Reflection 2: How should my life change if I live from the place of being chosen by God Himself?

____
____
____
____
____
____

Prayer: Lord, anchor me in the truth that I am chosen IN You. Pursued by You, not overlooked, forgotten or accidental, but intentionally selected & deeply desired, favoured & loved.

Day 1 *Chosen*

Day 2 *Accepted*

Scripture: Ephesians 1:6

"To the praise of the glory of His grace, by which He made us accepted in the Beloved."

Devotion:
In Christ, you are fully accepted—nothing to prove, nothing to earn. His approval is not based on your performance but on Jesus' finished work. Rest replaces striving when you understand this. When you live from this truth, insecurity begins to lose its grip. You no longer need to chase approval from others because you are secure in His approval and His acceptance.

Day 2 *Accepted*

Reflection 1: In what areas do I still seek approval?

____

____

____

____

____

____

Reflection 2: What would it look like to rest in God today?

____

____

____

____

____

____

Prayer: Lord, thank You that I am fully accepted in You. Help me release every need for approval and rest in Your grace. Let my life flow from the security of belonging to You.

Day 2 *Accepted*

Day 3 *Made New*

Scripture: 2 Corinthians 5:17

"Therefore, if anyone is in Christ, he is a new creation; old things have passed away; behold, all things have become new."

Devotion:

Your past no longer defines you; Christ has made you new. You are not being patched up—you are recreated. Step into the freedom of your new identity. Your identity is now found in Christ. He doesn't just improve your life; He gives you a completely new one. A consecrated life walks in this reality daily. As you surrender to Him, you step further into who He has already made you to be. You are no longer bound to old patterns—you are free to live fully in the newness of life IN HIM.

Day 3 *Made New*

Reflection 1: Am I still holding onto parts of my old identity?

____
____
____
____
____
____

Reflection 2: What does it look like for me to walk in newness today?

____
____
____
____
____
____

Prayer: Lord, thank You that I am made new in You. Help me release the past and step fully into the life You have given me. Let my thoughts, actions, and identity reflect this new creation.

Day 3 *Made New*

Day 4 *Loved*

Scripture: Jeremiah 31:3

"The Lord has appeared of old to me, saying: "Yes, I have loved you with an everlasting love; Therefore with lovingkindness I have drawn you.""

Devotion:

God's love for you is not temporary or based on your behaviour—it is unconditional and everlasting. His love pursues you, sustains you, and transforms you. It is a love that gives, a love without judgement, a love that is kind, a love that protects, a love that is patient.

His love for you is not small or distant—it is abundant, intentional, and personal. He has lavished His love upon you. When you truly receive it, everything begins to change.

Day 4 *Loved*

Reflection 1: Do I believe God loves me personally and deeply?

____

____

____

____

____

____

Reflection 2: What lies do I believe that oppose this truth?

____

____

____

____

____

____

Prayer: Father, thank You for Your overwhelming love for me. Let Your love sink deep into my heart. Help me receive it fully and live from it daily. Let Your love shape my identity and flow through my life to others.

Day 4 *Loved*

Day 5 *Secure*

Scripture: Proverbs 18:10

"The name of the Lord is a fortified tower; the righteous run to it and are safe."

Devotion:
There is nothing in all creation that can separate you from God's love. Even in your weakness, when life feels uncertain, His grip on you remains strong. Your security is found in His faithfulness, not your consistency. He is your refuge, your covering, and your unshakable foundation, you are held firmly in His hands.
A consecrated life rests in this security. When you know you are safe in Him, fear loses its grip and trust begins to grow. You no longer strive to control everything—you rest in the One who holds everything together.

Day 5 *Secure*

Reflection 1: What fears challenge my sense of security?

____
____
____
____
____
____

Reflection 2: How can I trust God more deeply?

____
____
____
____
____
____

Prayer: Lord, You are my rock and my refuge. Help me rest in Your security and trust You in every circumstance. Let my heart be anchored in You, unshaken and at peace.

Day 5 *Secure*

Day 6 *Complete*

Scripture: Colossians 2:10

"And you are complete in Him, who is the head of all principality and power."

Devotion:

In Christ, you are already made complete—you have nothing missing and nothing lacking. The world may tell you to chase more, but God invites you to rest in what He has already given. He alone is all you need, He is all-sufficient.

You have the freedom of salvation, complete forgiveness, victory and security, access to all wisdom and knowledge. True fullness is found in Him alone, requiring no additional ritual or works, just remaining IN HIM and resting in the finished work of the cross.

Day 6 *Complete*

Reflection 1: Where do I feel incomplete or lacking?

____
____
____
____
____
____

Reflection 2: What would it look like to live content?

____
____
____
____
____
____

Prayer: Lord, thank You that I am complete in You. Help me stop striving for what I already have and rest in Your fullness. Let my life reflect the wholeness and peace that comes from being in You.

Day 6 *Complete*

Day 7 *Hidden*

Scripture: Colossians 3:3

"For you died, and your life is hidden with Christ in God."

Devotion:
Your life is hidden with Christ, safe in His presence and covered by His grace. Your old life has been buried. The Father no longer sees the old sinful life, He now sees a new creation hidden in Christ — in His image and likeness.
Even when life feels uncertain, your true identity remains secure in Him. You are held, protected, secure and known, your identity is anchored IN HIM. You are treasured and valued, safe and loved, dead to sin and alive IN HIM.

Day 7 *Hidden*

Reflection 1: Do I find my identity in what is seen or in who I am IN HIM?

Reflection 2: How can I cultivate a deeper "hidden life" with Him daily?

Prayer: Lord, thank You that my life is hidden in You. Help me rest in that place of security and intimacy. Draw me deeper into Your presence and shape me in the secret place..

Day 7 *Hidden*

Day 8 *Known*

Scripture: Psalm 139:1

"O Lord, You have searched me and known me."

Devotion:
To be known by God is both humbling and deeply comforting. He sees every part of you—the hidden thoughts, the quiet struggles, the unspoken desires—and yet He draws near with love, not rejection. You don't have to perform or pretend before Him; consecration begins when you allow Him full access to your heart.
Being known by God means surrendering the parts you would rather hide, it is an invitation into intimacy, where nothing is covered. In His knowing, you are not exposed to shame—you are invited into transformation.

Day 8 *Known*

Reflection 1: What areas of my life am I still hiding from God?

____

____

____

____

____

____

Reflection 2: Do I truly believe He knows me and still loves me?

____

____

____

____

____

____

Prayer: Lord, search my heart and reveal anything that is not aligned with You. I choose to open every part of my life to You—knowing that in being fully known, I am fully loved. Shape me, purify me, and draw me deeper into intimacy with You.

Day 8 *Known*

Day 9 *Intimacy*

Scripture: James 4:8

"Draw near to God and He will draw near to you."

Devotion:
Intimacy with God is not built through performance but through presence. It is found in the quiet moments where you choose to come close—where distractions fade and your heart turns toward Him alone. God is not distant; He is waiting for you to draw near.

Consecration deepens through intimacy. As you spend time with Him, He gently reveals His heart and transforms yours. The more you know Him, the more your life begins to reflect Him—because intimacy always leads to becoming more like HIM.

Day 9 *Intimacy*

Reflection 1: What is currently competing for my time with God?

____
____
____
____
____

Reflection 2: How can I intentionally create space to draw near to Him daily?

____
____
____
____
____

Prayer: Jesus, I choose to come close to You. Remove every distraction and draw my heart into deeper intimacy with You. Let my life flow from being with You, not just doing for You.

Day 9 *Intimacy*

Day 10 *Abide*

Scripture: John 15:4-5

"Abide in Me, and I in you… whoever abides in Me bears much fruit."

Devotion:

Abiding is not striving—it is staying. It is choosing to remain connected to Jesus in every moment, allowing His life to flow through you. Fruitfulness is not something you force; it is the natural result of a life that stays close to Him.

In a world that pushes you to do more, abiding calls you to be with Him first. As you remain in His presence, your heart is shaped, your desires are refined, and your life begins to reflect Him. Consecration is sustained not by effort, but by connection.

Day 10 *Abide*

Reflection 1: Am I striving to produce fruit, or abiding in Him?

Reflection 2: What helps me stay connected to Jesus throughout my day?

Prayer: Jesus, teach me to abide in You. Help me remain close in every moment, drawing my strength and life from You alone. Let my life bear fruit that comes from staying rooted in Your presence.

Day 10 *Abide*

CONSECRATED

Day 11 *Set Apart*

"Come out from among them And be separate, says the Lord. Do not touch what is unclean, And I will receive you."

Devotion:

To be set apart means your life no longer blends in with the patterns around you—it reflects the nature of God. You have been called out of darkness into His light, not just to be different outwardly, but to be transformed inwardly. Holiness is not about restriction; it is about belonging fully to Him. Consecration is the response to that calling. As you surrender your life, God shapes your desires, your choices, and your direction. Being set apart is not about isolation—it is about living distinctly, marked by His presence in everything you do.

Day 11 *Set Apart*

Reflection 1: Where in my life am I blending in instead of being set apart?

____
____
____
____
____
____

Reflection 2: What is God asking me to surrender so I can live more fully for Him?

____
____
____
____
____
____

Prayer: Lord, set my life apart for You. Align my heart, my thoughts, and my actions with Your holiness. Let my life reflect that I belong completely to You.

Day 11 *Set Apart*

Day 12 *Cleansed*

Scripture: 1 John 1:9

"If we confess our sins, He is faithful and just to forgive us our sins and to cleanse us from all unrighteousness."

Devotion:
God does not expose your heart to shame you—He reveals it to cleanse you. When you come honestly before Him, He meets you with mercy and restoration. Cleansing is not something you achieve; it is something you receive when you surrender. We are washed by the blood of Christ.
A consecrated life is marked by continual cleansing. As you allow Him to wash your heart, your thoughts, and your desires, you become more aligned with His nature. His cleansing doesn't just remove sin—it restores intimacy and renews your spirit.

Day 12 *Cleansed*

Reflection 1: Is there anything I need to bring honestly before God today?

____
____
____
____
____
____

Reflection 2: Do I believe God fully cleanses me, or do I hold onto guilt?

____
____
____
____
____
____

Prayer: Lord, I come before You openly and honestly. Cleanse my heart, my thoughts, and my desires, and restore me in Your presence. Thank You that in You I am made clean.

Day 12 *Cleansed*

Day 13 *Sanctified*

Scripture: 1 Thessalonians 4:3

"For this is the will of God, your sanctification..."

Devotion:

Sanctification is the ongoing work of God setting you apart and making you more like Jesus. It is not instant perfection, but a daily transformation as you yield to Him. As you walk with Him, He shapes your desires, refines your character, and aligns your life with His will.

A consecrated life embraces this process. You are not who you used to be, and you are not yet who you will become—but God is faithfully working in you. As you surrender, His holiness is formed in you, and your life begins to reflect His nature more clearly.

Day 13 *Sanctified*

Reflection 1: Where do I see God working in my life right now?

____
____
____
____
____
____

Reflection 2: Am I yielding to His process or resisting it?

____
____
____
____
____
____

Prayer: Lord, I surrender to Your work in me. Sanctify my heart, my thoughts, and my life, and make me more like You each day. I trust Your process and Your timing.

Day 13 *Sanctified*

Day 14 *Made Holy*

Scripture: Hebrews 12:14

"Pursue peace with all people, and holiness, without which no one will see the Lord."

Devotion:
Holiness is not about perfection—it is about being set apart for God and living in alignment with His nature. It flows from relationship, not religion. As you walk closely with Him, His holiness begins to shape your thoughts, your desires, and your actions.
A consecrated life pursues holiness daily. Not out of pressure, but out of love—because you belong to Him. The closer you draw to God, the more your life reflects His purity and presence, revealing Him to the world around you.

Day 14 *Made Holy*

Reflection 1: What areas of my life are not yet aligned with God's holiness?

____
____
____
____
____
____

Reflection 2: Am I pursuing holiness from love or obligation?

____
____
____
____
____
____

Prayer: Lord, draw me closer to You and shape my life in Your holiness. Align my heart, my thoughts, and my actions with Your nature. Let my life reflect that I belong fully to You.

Day 14 *Made Holy*

Day 15 *Refined*

Scripture: Malachi 3:3

"He will sit as a refiner and purifier of silver…"

Devotion:
Refining is not about destruction—it is about purification. God allows the fire not to harm you, but to remove what does not belong and reveal what is genuine. In the process, He is near, attentive, and intentional, shaping you into something pure and valuable.

Just like gold is refined in the fire and all the dross rises to the top, we must allow the Lord to scoop off what rises. Even in discomfort, God is working to strengthen your faith, purify your heart, and deepen your dependence on Him. What feels like pressure is often preparation for greater intimacy and purpose.

Day 15 *Refined*

Reflection 1: What might God be refining in my life right now?

Reflection 2: Am I resisting the process or trusting His hand?

Prayer: Lord, I trust You in the refining process. Remove anything in me that does not reflect You, and strengthen what remains. Let my life be purified and shaped for Your glory.

Day 15 *Refined*

Day 16 *Purified*

Scripture: Psalm 24:3-4

"Who may ascend the hill of the Lord? He who has clean hands and a pure heart."

Devotion:
Purity is the result of a life surrendered to God and shaped by His presence. It is not about outward appearance, but an inward reality where your heart, motives, and desires are aligned with Him. As you walk closely with God, He purifies you—removing what clouds your vision and drawing you into deeper clarity and intimacy.
A purified life carries His presence. When your heart is clean before Him, you begin to see Him more clearly and reflect Him more fully. This is the fruit of consecration—living with a heart that is fully His, free, and undivided.

Day 16 *Purified*

Reflection 1: Are there areas of my heart that need realignment with God?

Reflection 2: What does it look like for me to live with an undivided heart before Him?

Prayer: Lord, purify my heart and align my desires with Yours. Remove anything that hinders intimacy with You, and let my life reflect Your purity. I choose to live fully surrendered, completely Yours.

Day 16 *Purified*

Day 17 *Sacrifice*

Scripture: Romans 12:1

"Offer your bodies as a living sacrifice, holy and pleasing to God—this is your true and proper worship."

Devotion:
A living sacrifice is not a one-time offering—it is a daily surrender. It means placing your life, your desires, your plans, and your will on the altar before God and choosing Him again and again. True worship is not just what you sing; it is how you live fully yielded to Him.
Consecration is lived out in the everyday moments. As you continually surrender, God shapes your life into something holy and pleasing to Him. What you give up is never lost—it is transformed in His hands into something far greater.

Day 17 *Sacrifice*

Reflection 1: What area of my life do I need to place on the altar today?

Reflection 2: What does daily surrender look like in my routine?

Prayer: Lord, I offer my life to You as a living sacrifice. Take every part of me—my thoughts, my desires, my plans—and align them with Your will. Let my life be an offering that brings You glory.

Day 17 *Sacrifice*

Day 18 *Renewed*

Scripture: Romans 12:2

"Be transformed by the renewing of your mind."

Devotion:
Renewal begins in the mind. As you allow God to reshape your thinking, your life begins to align with His truth instead of the patterns of the world. Old mindsets are replaced with His perspective, bringing clarity, peace, and transformation.
A consecrated life continually returns to this place of renewal. As you fill your heart and mind with His Word, replacing lies with His truth — He restores your vision, strengthens your faith, and leads you into His will. Renewal is not a one-time moment—it is a daily exchange for His truth.

Day 18 *Renewed*

Reflection 1: What thoughts or patterns need to be renewed in my mind?

____
____
____
____
____
____

Reflection 2: What truth from God's Word can I replace them with?

____
____
____
____
____
____

Prayer: Lord, renew my mind and align my thoughts with Your truth. Remove every pattern that does not reflect You, and fill me with Your perspective. Transform my life as I walk in Your will.

Day 18 *Renewed*

Day 19 *Disciplined*

Scripture: 2 Timothy 1:7

"For God has not given us a spirit of fear and timidity, but of power, love, and self-discipline."

Devotion:
Discipline is not restriction—it is alignment. It is choosing what leads you closer to God over what pulls you away, even when it's not easy. Through the Holy Spirit, you have been given self-control to live a life that reflects Him.
When you full consecrate yourself to God, you are formed and molded in the daily decisions no one else sees. As you practice discipline in your time with God, your thoughts, and your actions, you create space for Him to shape you. What begins as intentional effort becomes a lifestyle of devotion.

Day 19 *Disciplined*

Reflection 1: Where is God calling me to grow in discipline?

____
____
____
____
____
____

Reflection 2: What small daily habit can I start or strengthen today?

____
____
____
____
____
____

Prayer: Lord, strengthen me to live a disciplined life that honours You. Help me choose what leads me closer to You each day. Form in me a life of consistency, obedience, and devotion.

Day 19 *Disciplined*

Day 20 *Surrendered*

Scripture: Luke 22:42

"Not my will, but Yours be done."

Devotion:
Surrender is trust — trusting that God has the best plans for your life. It is choosing God's will over your own, even when it costs something. In surrender, you release control and place your life fully into His hands, trusting that His way is better.
A consecrated life is marked by continual surrender. As you lay down your plans, your desires, and your expectations, God replaces them with His purpose and peace. What you surrender to Him is never wasted —it is transformed for His glory.

Day 20 *Surrendered*

Reflection 1: What am I holding onto that God is asking me to surrender?

____
____
____
____
____

Reflection 2: Do I trust God enough to let go of control?

____
____
____
____
____

Prayer: Lord, I surrender my will to Yours. Take every part of my life and align it with Your purpose. Teach me to trust You fully and walk in obedience to Your leading.

Day 20 *Surrendered*

TRANSFORMED

&

EMPOWERED

Day 21 *Established*

Scripture: 2 Corinthians 1:21

"Now He who establishes us with you in Christ and has anointed us is God."

Devotion:
It is God who establishes you, not your own strength or effort. You don't have to hold yourself together — He does! He is the one who steadies your steps and confirms your calling. As you lean on Him, your life becomes firm and unshaken. He is your firm foundation, the cornerstone.
A consecrated life is grounded in this truth. As you remain in Him, He strengthens, steadies, and roots you deeply. You are not easily shaken, because your life is established by God Himself.

Day 21 *Established*

Reflection 1: What areas of my life are unstable?

____
____
____
____
____
____

Reflection 2: How can I allow God to establish me
more deeply IN HIM?

____
____
____
____
____

Prayer: Lord, establish my life firmly in You.
Strengthen my foundation and help me stand strong
in every season. Let my life be rooted and unshaken in
Christ.

Day 21 *Established*

Day 22 *Confident*

Scripture: Hebrews 4:6

"Let us then approach God's throne of grace with confidence."

Devotion:

Confidence in God is not based on who you are in yourself, but who you are IN HIM. Because of Jesus, you can come boldly before God—fully known, fully accepted, and fully loved. There is no hesitation, no fear, only access to His grace and mercy.
A consecrated life walks in this confidence daily. As you remain in Him, insecurity fades and boldness grows—not in pride, but in trust. You don't shrink back; you step forward, knowing you are held, led, and empowered by Him.

Day 22 *Confident*

Reflection 1: Do I approach God with confidence or hesitation?

____
____
____
____
____
____

Reflection 2: What would change if I truly believed I have full access to Him?

____
____
____
____
____
____

Prayer: Lord, thank You that I can come to You with confidence. Strengthen my heart to walk boldly in who You have called me to be. Let my life reflect trust, courage, and faith in You.

Day 22 *Confident*

Day 23 *Purpose*

Scripture: Ephesians 2:10

"For we are His workmanship, created in Christ Jesus for good works, which God prepared beforehand."

Devotion:
Your life is not random—you were intentionally created by God with purpose. Before you ever took a step, He had already prepared a path for you to walk in. Purpose is not something you strive to find; it is something you discover as you walk closely with Him. As you continue to live a consecrated life you will align with that purpose. As you surrender and follow His leading, He reveals the assignments, the moments, and the people He has placed before you. Purpose unfolds in obedience—one step at a time—as you live fully IN HIM.

Day 23 *Purpose*

Reflection 1: Do I trust that God has a purpose for my life?

____

____

____

____

____

Reflection 2: What step of obedience is He asking me to take right now?

____

____

____

____

____

Prayer: Lord, thank You that my life has purpose in You. Lead me in the path You have prepared, and give me the courage to walk in it. Let my life reflect Your plans and bring You glory.

Day 23 *Purpose*

Day 24 *Strengthened*

Scripture: Phillipians 4:13

"I can do all things through Christ who strengthens me."

Devotion:
Your strength is not found in your own ability, but in Christ who lives within you. When you feel weak, overwhelmed, or stretched, He meets you with grace and fills you with His power. You were never meant to carry life on your own—His strength sustains you. A consecrated life learns to depend on Him daily. As you surrender your limitations, He releases His strength, enabling you to stand firm, endure, and move forward with confidence. In Him, weakness becomes the place where His power is revealed.

Day 24 *Strengthened*

Reflection 1: Where do I feel weak or overwhelmed right now?

____
____
____
____
____
____

Reflection 2: How can I lean on God's strength instead of my own?

____
____
____
____
____
____

Prayer: Lord, I receive Your strength today. In my weakness, be my power and my support. Help me walk forward with confidence, knowing that You are sustaining me.

Day 24 *Strengthened*

Day 25 *Fruitful*

Scripture: John 15:8

"This is to My Father's glory, that you bear much fruit, showing yourselves to be My disciples."

Devotion:
Fruitfulness is the evidence of a life connected to Jesus. It is not something you force or manufacture—it flows naturally as you abide in Him. As His life fills you, it produces love, peace, patience, goodness, and a life that reflects His nature.
As you remain surrendered and aligned with Him, your life begins to impact others in ways you may not even see. Your live will bear fruit that brings glory to God. Fruitfulness is not about striving—it is about staying close.

Day 25 *Fruitful*

Reflection 1: What fruit is currently growing in my life?

____

____

____

____

____

____

Reflection 2: How can I stay connected to Jesus so fruit continues to grow?

____

____

____

____

____

____

Prayer: Lord, let my life bear fruit that reflects You. Help me remain close to You so that Your life flows through me. May everything I do bring glory to You.

Day 25 *Fruitful*

Day 26 *Overflow*

Scripture: Ephesians 3:20

"Now to Him who is able to do immeasurably more than all we ask or imagine."

Devotion:
God's desire is not just to fill your life, but to cause it to overflow. When you live consecrated and connected to Him, His presence, peace, and power begin to spill over into every area of your life. What He pours into you is never meant to stay contained—it is meant to flow outward, like a gushing river!
A life surrendered to Him becomes a vessel of overflow. As you remain in Him, others begin to encounter His love through you. Overflow is the fruit of intimacy, alignment, and surrender—a life so filled with God that it cannot help but pour out.

Day 26 *Overflow*

Reflection 1: What is God pouring into my life right now?

____
____
____
____
____
____

Reflection 2: How can I allow His presence to flow through me to others?

____
____
____
____
____
____

Prayer: Lord, fill me to overflowing. Let Your presence, love, and power flow through my life to those around me. Use me as a vessel that carries Your glory and changes the atmosphere wherever I go.

Day 26 *Overflow*

Day 27 *Bold*

Scripture: Proverbs 28:1

"The righteous are as bold as a lion."

Devotion:
Boldness in God is not loud confidence—it is quiet certainty in who He is and who you are IN HIM. When you know you are His, fear begins to lose its grip, and courage rises within you. Boldness is not about personality; it is about identity.
A consecrated life walks with holy boldness. As you remain surrendered to God, He gives you the courage to speak, to step out, and to live unashamed for Him. You are not called to shrink back—you are called to stand firm and shine.

Day 27 *Bold*

Reflection 1: Where is fear holding me back from being bold?

____

____

____

____

____

____

Reflection 2: What step of faith is God asking me to take?

____

____

____

____

____

____

Prayer: Father, give me boldness that comes from You. Help me stand firm in my identity and walk in courage. Let my life reflect fearless faith and trust in You.

Day 27 *Bold*

Day 28 *Perseverance*

Scripture: Hebrews 12:1

"Let us run with perseverance the race marked out for us."

Devotion:

Perseverance is the strength to keep going, even when the journey feels long or difficult. In Christ, you are not running alone—He is with you, strengthening you and guiding your steps. What God has begun in you, He is faithful to complete.

A consecrated life is marked by endurance. As you remain anchored in Him, you develop resilience that carries you through every season. Perseverance is not just about finishing—it is about staying faithful along the way.

Day 28 *Perseverance*

Reflection 1: Is there an area in my life where I feel like giving up right now?

____
____
____
____
____
____

Reflection 2: How can I rely on God to persevere in this area?

____
____
____
____
____
____

Prayer: Father, strengthen me to persevere in every season. Help me stay faithful, even when it's hard. Remind me that You are with me, and give me endurance to finish the race You have set before me.

Day 28 *Perseverance*

Day 29 *Commissioned*

Scripture: John 20:21

"As the Father has sent Me, I am sending you."

Devotion:
You have not only been set apart—you have been sent. Everything God has done in you—cleansing, refining, transforming—has prepared you to carry His presence into the world. Your life is now a vessel of His love, truth, and power.
A consecrated life does not remain hidden; it is commissioned for purpose. As you go, you carry His authority, His Spirit, and His heart for others. You are not sent in your own strength—you go IN HIM, empowered and led by Him.

Day 29 *Commissioned*

Reflection 1: Where is God sending me in this season?

____
____
____
____
____
____

Reflection 2: How can I reflect Him in my everyday life?

____
____
____
____
____

Prayer: Lord, I receive Your call to go. Send me where You desire, and use my life for Your glory. Let me carry Your presence and reflect Your heart in everything I do.

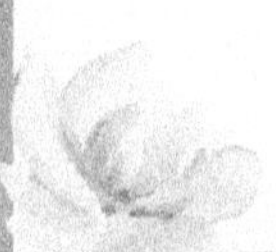

Day 29 *Commissioned*

Day 30 *Fullness*

Scripture: Ephesians 4:13

"Till we all come to the unity of the faith and of the knowledge of the Son of God, to a perfect man, to the measure of the stature of the fullness of Christ."

Devotion:

Over the month, God has been drawing you deeper—cleansing, refining, aligning, and transforming your life. What began as surrender has become intimacy; what began as consecration has become identity. Now you stand not empty, but filled—carrying His presence, shaped by His hand, and established IN HIM.

Fullness is not the end of the journey—it is the beginning of a life lived in Him. You are no longer striving to become; you are living from who you are in Christ. As you continue walking with Him, His grace will continue to flow, His presence will continue to fill, and your life will continue to overflow with His glory.

Day 30 *Fullness*

Reflection 1: What has God done in my heart and life over these past 30 days?

____
____
____
____
____
____

Reflection 2: How will I continue to live from His fullness moving forward?

____
____
____
____
____
____

Prayer: Lord, thank You for all You have done in me. Thank You for consecrating my life and filling me with Your presence. I choose to continue walking with You, living from Your fullness, and reflecting Your glory in everything I do.

Day 30 *Fullness*